Home

Fabiola Sepulveda

Notes for the Grown-ups

This wordless book allows for a rich shared reading experience for children who do not yet know how to read words or who are beginning to learn. Children can look at the pages to gather information from what they see, and they can suggest text to tell the story.

To extend this reading experience, do one or more of the following:

Share with each other what home means to you.

Introduce vocabulary such as these words when looking at the pictures and telling the story you see:

- bathroom
- bed
- bedroom
- chair
- closet
- door
- home
- kitchen
- mailbox
- patio
- sink
- table
- window
- yard

Talk about the different types of homes people have.

After reading the pictures, come back to the book again and again. Rereading is an excellent tool for building literacy skills.

Ask the child to draw a picture showing their favorite thing about their home.

Consultant

Cynthia Malo, M.A.Ed.

Publishing Credits

Rachelle Cracchiolo, M.S.Ed., *Publisher*
Emily R. Smith, M.A.Ed., *SVP of Content Development*
Véronique Bos, *VP of Creative*
Dona Herweck Rice, *Senior Content Manager*

Image Credits: all images from iStock and/or Shutterstock

Library of Congress Cataloging-in-Publication Data
Names: Sepulveda, Fabiola, author.
Title: Home / Fabiola Sepulveda.
Description: Huntington Beach, CA : TCM, Teacher Created Materials, [2024]
| Audience: Ages 3-9 | Summary: "Many things make a home. Doors,
windows, and furniture are some of those things. What makes a home for
you?"-- Provided by publisher.
Identifiers: LCCN 2024007554 (print) | LCCN 2024007555 (ebook) | ISBN
9798765961278 (paperback) | ISBN 9798765967492 (ebook)
Subjects: LCSH: Dwellings--Juvenile literature.
Classification: LCC TH4811.5 .S47 2024 (print) | LCC TH4811.5 (ebook) |
DDC 643/.1--dc23/eng/20240304
LC record available at https://lccn.loc.gov/2024007554
LC ebook record available at https://lccn.loc.gov/2024007555

TCM Teacher Created Materials

5482 Argosy Avenue
Huntington Beach, CA 92649
www.tcmpub.com
ISBN 979-8-7659-6127-8
© 2025 Teacher Created Materials, Inc.
Printed by: 926. Printed in: Malaysia. PO#: PO11723